Chapter 1: Active Introductions

In today's world, information is power. Governments, corporations, and individuals are constantly seeking to shape the narrative and influence outcomes in their favor. From political campaigns to business negotiations, the ability to persuade and manipulate is a critical skill.

In this instalment of Essential Tradecraft, we will be exploring two related but distinct areas of influence: Influence Tactics and Active Measures. Both involve the use of information and psychological manipulation to achieve a desired outcome, but they operate at different scales and with different levels of visibility.

Influence Tactics are the more subtle and everyday techniques used to persuade and influence others. From the way we dress and speak, to the stories we tell and the arguments we make, Influence Tactics are part of our everyday interactions. They can be used for both good and bad, and their effectiveness depends on the skill of the user and the receptivity of the target.

Active Measures, on the other hand, are a more covert and aggressive form of influence. They involve the use of deception, disinformation, and propaganda to shape the opinions and actions of a target population. Active Measures can be used to sow confusion, create division, and even manipulate the outcomes of elections and other critical events. They are often associated with espionage and covert operations, but can also be employed by non-state actors and individuals.

Throughout this book, we will explore both Influence Tactics and Active Measures in detail, examining their history, their methods, and their ethical implications. We will provide practical guidance and advice on how to use these techniques effectively and responsibly, while also raising awareness of their potential risks and drawbacks.

Ultimately, the goal of this book is to help readers understand the power of influence, and to equip them with the knowledge and tools to navigate this complex and ever-changing landscape. Whether you are a business professional, a political campaigner, or simply interested in the art of persuasion, Essential Tradecraft: Influence Tactics and Active Measures is an essential resource for mastering the art of influence.

Chapter 2: Influence Campaigns

Influence campaigns have been used for centuries by governments, organizations, and individuals to shape public opinion, sway elections, and advance their interests. These campaigns involve the use of various tactics, such as propaganda, disinformation, and psychological operations, to influence people's attitudes and behaviors.

The goal of an Influence campaign is to change the way people think or act in a way that benefits the campaign's sponsor. The techniques used in these campaigns have become increasingly sophisticated over time, with the rise of technology and the advent of social media providing new avenues for influence.

Influence campaigns have been used by a range of actors throughout history, from monarchs seeking to bolster their legitimacy to governments attempting to rally their citizens during wartime. In recent years, influence campaigns have come to the forefront of public attention due to their role in shaping political events, particularly during elections.

The effectiveness of Influence campaigns depends on understanding the psychology of how people make decisions and form opinions. The following psychological principles are often used in influence campaigns:

Social Proof: People tend to conform to the behavior of those around them. This is why advertisers use testimonials and celebrity endorsements to sell products.

Reciprocity: People feel a sense of obligation to return a favor. Influence campaigns may use this principle by offering gifts or other incentives in exchange for support.

Authority: People are more likely to follow the advice of someone they perceive as an authority. Influence campaigns may use this principle by using experts or influential figures to endorse a particular message or cause.

Scarcity: People tend to place a higher value on things that are rare or in short supply. Influence campaigns may use this principle by creating a sense of urgency or scarcity around a particular message or cause.

Consistency: People prefer to be consistent in their attitudes and behaviors. Influence campaigns may use this principle by getting people to make small commitments to a cause or message, which can then be built upon over time.

Liking: People are more likely to be influenced by those they like and find attractive. Influence campaigns may use this principle by using attractive or likeable spokespeople to deliver a message or by creating a sense of community around a particular cause.

Understanding these principles can help individuals and organizations create effective influence campaigns. However, it is important to note that some of these principles can be manipulative and unethical if used improperly. As such, it is important to use these principles with care and consideration for the well-being and autonomy of the individuals being influenced.

Influence campaigns have been used throughout history to manipulate public opinion and sway decision-making processes. Here are a few notable examples of influence campaigns from different parts of the world:

Operation INFEKTION: This was a disinformation campaign initiated by the KGB in the 1980s to spread the false claim that the United States had created HIV/AIDS in order to target African Americans and gay men. The campaign was intended to create discord and mistrust towards the United States.

Brexit: During the UK's referendum on leaving the European Union, several influence campaigns were detected. For example, the Russian government was accused of using social media bots to spread anti-EU messages, while the Vote Leave campaign was accused of breaking electoral law by exceeding spending limits.

Arab Spring: Social media played a critical role in the uprisings that took place across North Africa and the Middle East during the Arab Spring. The use of social media allowed protesters to organize and disseminate information outside the control of traditional state-run media outlets, which had previously maintained a monopoly on information.

Cambridge Analytica: This was a British political consulting firm that was hired by the Trump campaign during the 2016 US Presidential election. The firm used data mining and targeted advertising to influence voter behavior and ultimately sway the election in Trump's favor.

These examples highlight the diverse range of techniques and methods used in influence campaigns, as well as the political, social, and economic implications of such campaigns.

In recent years, there have been several high-profile cases of alleged influence campaigns carried out by foreign actors. While the specific details and perpetrators are often contested and debated, what is clear is that influence campaigns have become an increasingly prevalent tactic in modern warfare, politics, and business.

The practice of Influence campaigns can be traced back centuries, with examples ranging from propaganda in World War I and II to covert operations during the Cold War. In the modern era, influence campaigns have evolved to leverage social media, big data, and sophisticated psychological techniques to manipulate public opinion and behavior.

One of the key components of an influence campaign is the target audience. The campaign aims to identify and exploit vulnerabilities in the audience, such as pre-existing beliefs, biases, fears, and desires. By tapping into these vulnerabilities, the campaign can sway the audience towards a particular viewpoint or action.

Another important aspect of influence campaigns is the messaging. The campaign aims to create persuasive and memorable messages that resonate with the target audience. These messages can take various forms, such as news articles, social media posts, memes, videos, or advertisements.

The methods used to distribute these messages can also vary widely. Some influence campaigns rely on bots and fake accounts to amplify their messaging, while others use legitimate media outlets or prominent individuals to spread their message.

In recent years, there has been growing awareness and concern about the impact of influence campaigns on democracy, national security, and individual autonomy. Efforts to combat these campaigns have included increased regulation of social media platforms, the development of counter-narratives and fact-checking initiatives, and improved education and awareness among the public.

Chapter 3: Active Measures

Active Measures have been an integral part of espionage and intelligence operations since the early days of the Cold War. The Soviet Union, in particular, is known for developing and implementing active measures as a tool for achieving strategic objectives. Active Measures are a type of covert operation that seeks to influence political and social outcomes in foreign countries through a variety of means, including propaganda, disinformation, and other covert actions. These measures are often used to sow discord, undermine confidence in democratic institutions, and promote the interests of the state conducting the operation.

The history of Active Measures can be traced back to the early days of the Soviet Union. In the 1920s and 1930s, Soviet intelligence agencies began using propaganda and disinformation campaigns to influence political and social developments in foreign countries. During World War II, Soviet intelligence agents also engaged in sabotage and other covert operations to disrupt Nazi operations in Europe.

After the war, the Soviet Union continued to develop and refine its active measures capabilities. The KGB, the Soviet intelligence agency responsible for conducting active measures, developed a sophisticated network of agents, front organizations, and media outlets to promote Soviet interests abroad. The KGB used active measures to sow discord in Western democracies, to undermine the credibility of Western institutions, and to promote Soviet-style communism around the world.

One of the most well-known examples of Soviet active measures was the disinformation campaign aimed at discrediting the United States and its allies during the 1980s. The KGB and other Soviet intelligence agencies spread rumors and false information about a range of topics, including the AIDS epidemic, U.S. foreign policy, and the arms race. These efforts were designed to sow doubt and confusion in the minds of Western citizens and to undermine confidence in their governments and institutions.

Today, active measures continue to be used by intelligence agencies around the world. While the tactics and techniques may have evolved over time, the basic objectives remain the same: to influence political and social outcomes in foreign countries in order to advance the interests of the state conducting the operation. Understanding the history and practice of active measures is essential for anyone involved in the field of intelligence or international relations.

The Soviet Union was known for its extensive use of Active Measures as part of its foreign policy. Soviet Active Measures were part of the KGB's (Soviet Union's intelligence agency) covert operations, and their primary aim was to weaken Western democracies and influence public opinion.

One of the most well-known Soviet Active Measures campaigns was Operation INFEKTION, which began in the 1980s. The campaign was designed to discredit the United States by spreading the rumor that the AIDS virus was created in a U.S. government laboratory. The KGB used a combination of disinformation tactics, such as planting articles in foreign newspapers and creating forged documents to support the claim. The campaign was successful in spreading the rumor and damaging the reputation of the U.S. in the eyes of many.

Another example of Soviet Active Measures was the "Operation Trust" campaign, which was designed to manipulate the White Army during the Russian Civil War in the 1920s. The KGB created a fake anti-Bolshevik organization, which they convinced the White Army was real. The KGB then used this fake organization to pass disinformation and sow discord within the White Army, ultimately leading to its defeat.

Soviet Active Measures were not limited to disinformation campaigns but also included covert operations such as assassinations, kidnappings, and bombings. These tactics were used by the KGB to eliminate political opponents and silence dissidents both within the Soviet Union and abroad.

Active Measures can be divided into various techniques, each designed to achieve a specific objective. Here are some of the most commonly used Active Measures techniques:

Disinformation: The spreading of false or misleading information to influence public opinion or decision-making.

Propaganda: The use of biased or misleading information, images, and messages to manipulate public opinion.

Agent of influence: A person or group that is recruited or influenced by a foreign power to act in their interests.

Compromising material: The use of blackmail, bribery, or other forms of leverage to coerce individuals or groups to act in a particular way.

Forgeries: The creation of false documents, identities, or other materials to deceive or manipulate individuals or organizations.

Front organizations: The creation of fake organizations or businesses to provide cover for illegal activities or to influence political or social outcomes.

Cyber attacks: The use of computer hacking, malware, and other forms of cyber warfare to disrupt or influence government, corporate, or military operations.

These techniques can be used in combination with each other to create a more comprehensive Active Measures campaign. For example, a disinformation campaign may involve the use of fake news stories and propaganda, as well as the recruitment of agents of influence to spread the false information. Similarly, a cyber attack may be used to steal compromising material, which can then be used to blackmail or influence individuals or groups.

It Is important to note that Active Measures are not always used for nefarious purposes. In some cases, they may be used for legitimate intelligence gathering or to counter foreign influence operations. However, when used with malicious intent, Active Measures can be extremely effective in achieving a foreign power's objectives while remaining difficult to detect or attribute.

During the Cold War, the Soviet Union and the United States engaged in a global struggle for political and ideological dominance. As part of this struggle, both sides employed active measures in an effort to influence and manipulate foreign governments and populations.

The Soviet Union was particularly active in this regard, using a wide range of active measures to advance its interests and undermine those of its adversaries. These measures included disinformation campaigns, propaganda efforts, and covert operations aimed at destabilizing governments or interfering in their internal affairs.

One of the most well-known examples of Soviet active measures during the Cold War was Operation INFEKTION. This was a disinformation campaign launched in the 1980s that falsely claimed that the AIDS virus had been created by the United States as a biological weapon. The campaign was intended to sow distrust of the United States and create divisions within the Western alliance.

The United States also engaged in active measures during the Cold War, although to a lesser extent than the Soviet Union. One example of US active measures was the covert operation to fund and support the Solidarity movement in Poland in the 1980s. This effort was intended to undermine the communist government in Poland and promote democratic reforms.

The Cold War era saw a significant expansion in the use of active measures by both the Soviet Union and the United States. Many of the tactics and techniques developed during this period are still in use today, as countries continue to seek to influence and manipulate foreign governments and populations for strategic gain.

Chapter 4: Information

In today's fast-paced information age, the ability to distinguish between reliable information and propaganda is crucial. Misinformation, disinformation, and malformation are three common techniques used to manipulate public opinion, sow confusion, and further hidden agendas. Understanding the differences between these techniques is essential for anyone seeking to navigate the complex landscape of modern information warfare.

Misinformation is the dissemination of false or inaccurate information with the intention of deceiving or misleading people. Misinformation can be spread intentionally or unintentionally and can be motivated by a variety of factors, including political ideology, financial gain, or personal beliefs. Misinformation can take many forms, including fake news stories, rumors, and misleading statistics.

Disinformation, on the other hand, is the intentional spread of false or misleading information with the aim of manipulating public opinion or advancing a particular agenda. Unlike misinformation, which can be spread inadvertently, disinformation is always a deliberate attempt to deceive or mislead. Disinformation can be used to spread conspiracy theories, defame political opponents, or promote a particular ideology.

Malformation is a more subtle form of information manipulation, which involves selectively presenting information in a way that creates a distorted view of reality. Malformation is often used to reinforce existing biases or prejudices, or to create a false sense of consensus around a particular issue. Malformation can be used in a variety of contexts, from political advertising to media coverage of current events.

There are several types of misinformation that can be spread through influence campaigns or active measures. These include:

Propaganda: Propaganda is a type of information that is used to influence an audience's beliefs or actions. It often presents a biased or one-sided view of a topic, and is designed to appeal to the emotions rather than reason. Propaganda can be spread through various media channels, including print, broadcast, and social media.

Rumors: Rumors are unverified pieces of information that are spread through word of mouth. They often rely on emotional appeal and can be difficult to debunk once they have gained traction.

Hoaxes: Hoaxes are deliberately fabricated pieces of information that are designed to deceive people. They can be spread through various media channels, and are often created for entertainment or malicious purposes.

Fake News: Fake news is a type of misinformation that is presented as if it were real news. It can be spread through social media, news websites, and other media channels.

Misleading Statistics: Misleading statistics are statistics that are presented in a way that distorts the truth. They can be used to support a particular viewpoint or agenda, and can be spread through various media channels.

Disinformation refers to the deliberate spreading of false or misleading information with the intent to deceive. It is often used as a tactic in influence campaigns and active measures. Disinformation can take many forms, including fabricated stories, manipulated images and videos, and misleading or distorted information.

Disinformation campaigns can be carried out by a variety of actors, including governments, political parties, and other organizations. The goal of these campaigns is often to undermine the credibility of their opponents, sow discord and confusion, and shape public opinion.

One common tactic used in disinformation campaigns is the creation of fake social media accounts and the use of bots to amplify false narratives. These accounts are designed to appear legitimate and often use stolen identities or fake personas to make them harder to detect.

Another tactic is the use of propaganda, which involves the dissemination of information designed to promote a particular agenda or point of view. Propaganda can be spread through a variety of channels, including news outlets, social media, and advertising.

The effects of disinformation can be far-reaching, causing harm to individuals, organizations, and even entire societies.

There are various techniques that can be used to spread misinformation, disinformation, and malformation. Here are a few:

Fabrication: This involves creating false information and passing it off as real. This can be done through the creation of fake news articles, social media posts, or even fake websites.

Manipulation: This involves taking true information and manipulating it in a way that changes the message. This can be done through selective editing, taking quotes out of context, or twisting the facts to fit a particular narrative.

Amplification: This involves taking a piece of information and amplifying it to a point where it becomes the dominant narrative. This can be done through the use of social media, where a small piece of information can quickly spread and become a trending topic.

Repetition: This involves repeating a piece of information over and over again until it becomes ingrained in people's minds. This can be done through the use of slogans, catchphrases, or even memes.

Inoculation: This involves providing people with a small amount of misinformation in order to inoculate them against a larger dose of misinformation that may be presented later. This can be done by presenting a false argument and then debunking it, in order to build up people's resistance to similar arguments in the future.

These techniques are often used in combination with one another in order to create a powerful and persuasive message. They can be used to sway public opinion, discredit opponents, or promote a particular agenda.

Malformation refers to the deliberate manipulation of information in order to create confusion or mislead people. Unlike disinformation and misinformation, which are based on false information, malformation is based on a distortion of facts that are partially or completely true. The goal of malformation is not necessarily to create a specific belief or perception, but rather to create confusion and mistrust.

There are different techniques of malformation that can be used to achieve this goal. One of the most common is to selectively highlight certain facts while ignoring others, thus creating an incomplete and distorted picture of a situation. Another technique is to present a large amount of information that is loosely connected, making it difficult for the audience to identify the main message or to distinguish between fact and opinion.

Malformation can be particularly effective in situations where the audience has limited knowledge or expertise on the subject matter. In such cases, even a small amount of distortion or manipulation can have a significant impact on the audience's perception and understanding of the issue.

Malformation can be seen in various fields, such as politics, business, and media. For example, a political candidate might selectively highlight certain aspects of their opponent's record while ignoring others, creating an incomplete picture of their opponent's performance. Similarly, a company might release a large amount of data about its product, making it difficult for consumers to identify the most important features and make informed decisions. In media, malformation can be used to create sensationalist headlines that misrepresent the underlying story.

In the context of covert operations, malformation can be used to create confusion and mistrust among the target audience. By distorting or manipulating information, the operator can create doubt and uncertainty, making it difficult for the target to make informed decisions or to trust the information they receive. This can be particularly effective in situations where the target is under stress or pressure, such as during a crisis or conflict.

Malformation is another form of information warfare where the goal is to distort or manipulate information to create confusion or chaos. Malformation techniques may involve altering the context of information or creating entirely false information to sow doubt and uncertainty in the target audience.

One common example of malformation is the use of deepfake videos. Deepfakes are manipulated videos that use artificial intelligence to superimpose one person's face onto another person's body or make them say or do things they never actually did. Deepfakes can be used to spread false information and manipulate public opinion.

Another example of malformation is the use of fake social media accounts or bots to amplify certain messages or to create the illusion of popular support for a particular cause or ideology. These tactics are often used by state-sponsored actors or political campaigns to manipulate public opinion.

Malformation tactics can be particularly difficult to combat, as they often involve the creation of entirely false information. It is important for individuals and organizations to stay vigilant and to verify the sources of information before accepting it as true.

Misinformation, disinformation, and malformation are all powerful tools of influence and active measures. By understanding these tactics and how they are used, individuals and organizations can better protect themselves from the effects of information warfare.

Chapter 5: Credibility

Creating credibility is an essential aspect of any successful psychological operation. When attempting to influence an audience, it is critical to establish trust and reliability, and to present a convincing argument that can withstand scrutiny. To achieve this, it is important to carefully consider the audience's beliefs, values, and expectations, and to craft a message that resonates with them on a personal level.

One of the most effective ways to create credibility is to use social proof, which is the psychological phenomenon that people tend to conform to the behavior and opinions of others in their social group. By demonstrating that a particular opinion or behavior is widely held, it becomes more likely that others will adopt that same opinion or behavior.

Social proof can be established in a variety of ways, such as by referencing the opinions of experts, celebrities, or other respected figures, or by presenting statistics that show a majority of people share a particular belief or attitude. It can also be established by leveraging the power of online reviews and ratings, which are increasingly influential in shaping public opinion.

However, it is important to note that social proof can also be manipulated and exploited, particularly in the age of social media, where bots and fake accounts can be used to create the illusion of popularity and support. As such, it is crucial to ensure that any social proof used in a psychological operation is genuine and verifiable, and that it accurately reflects the opinions and attitudes of the target audience.

Creating credibility is a multifaceted process that requires careful consideration of the audience, the message, and the medium through which it is delivered. By leveraging social proof and other persuasive techniques, it is possible to establish trust and reliability, and to craft a message that is both compelling and effective.

Another key aspect of creating credibility in messaging is consistency and repetition. Consistency ensures that the message being communicated is not contradictory or confusing, while repetition helps to reinforce the message and make it stick in the minds of the audience.

Consistency can be achieved by ensuring that the messaging is aligned with the values, beliefs, and interests of the target audience. This requires an understanding of the audience's preferences, behaviors, and motivations, as well as a deep knowledge of the cultural and social contexts in which they operate.

Repetition can be achieved through various means, including the use of catchy slogans, memorable visuals, and consistent messaging across different channels and platforms. However, it's important to balance repetition with variety to avoid boredom or fatigue among the audience.

Consistency and repetition are key components of creating credibility in messaging, as they help to establish a clear and coherent message that is both memorable and persuasive.

Another effective way to create credibility in messaging is to emphasize common goals and interests between the target audience and the source of the message. By doing so, the target audience is more likely to view the message as credible and in their best interest.

This technique involves conducting research on the target audience to identify their needs, concerns, and aspirations. Once this information is gathered, the message can be tailored to highlight how the goals of the target audience align with those of the message source.

For example, if the goal is to promote a specific product or service, the message can emphasize how it meets the needs of the target audience and addresses their concerns. If the goal is to promote a political agenda, the message can emphasize how it aligns with the values and aspirations of the target audience.

By emphasizing common goals and interests, the target audience is more likely to view the message as trustworthy and credible, leading to greater acceptance and support for the operation.

One effective way to build credibility is by using the expertise of recognized authorities or experts in the relevant field. People are more likely to trust a message if they believe it comes from a credible source. This can be achieved through the use of quotes, citations, or endorsements from authoritative figures.

For example, if a political campaign wants to promote a policy on climate change, they may use quotes or endorsements from reputable scientists, environmental groups, or policymakers to lend credibility to their message. Similarly, a company promoting a new product may use testimonials from industry experts or celebrities to bolster the product's reputation.

Another strategy for building credibility is by providing evidence to support claims. This can involve citing scientific studies, statistics, or other data to back up the claims being made. When people see that there is solid evidence to support a message, they are more likely to believe it.

It's Important to note, however, that the evidence presented must be accurate and unbiased.

Misrepresenting data or cherry-picking information to support a predetermined agenda can actually harm credibility and erode trust.

Creating credibility in messaging is a critical component of successful influence campaigns. By using authoritative sources and providing accurate evidence, operatives can build trust with their target audience and increase the effectiveness of their messages.

Consistency is key to building credibility and trustworthiness in messaging. When a message is consistent across various platforms, it helps create a sense of reliability and authenticity. A message should be consistent not only in its content but also in its tone, delivery, and timing. A consistent message reinforces the idea that the source is reliable and trustworthy.

Inconsistencies in messaging, on the other hand, can lead to confusion and mistrust. For example, if a message is delivered with one tone on one platform and a different tone on another platform, it can create doubts about the source's authenticity. Similarly, if a message contradicts previous messages or is inconsistent with the source's previous positions, it can undermine the source's credibility and trustworthiness.

To ensure consistency in messaging, it is important to establish clear guidelines and protocols for communication. This includes guidelines for tone, style, and content of messaging, as well as guidelines for the timing and frequency of messaging. It is also important to have a central authority or point of contact responsible for coordinating and approving messaging across various platforms. By maintaining consistency in messaging, a source can build credibility and trustworthiness with its audience, enhancing the effectiveness of its operation.

Social proof is a psychological phenomenon in which people look to the behavior of others to guide their own actions. It can be a powerful tool in creating credibility and trustworthiness in messaging. By demonstrating that other people, particularly those who are respected or influential, believe or act in a certain way, it can increase the perceived legitimacy and effectiveness of the message.

One way to use social proof is to highlight the support of well-respected individuals or organizations. For example, a statement by a respected scientist or expert in a particular field can add credibility to a message on a related topic. Similarly, endorsements from respected organizations or institutions can enhance the perceived legitimacy of a message.

Another way to use social proof is to highlight the actions of others. For example, if a particular behavior or action is presented as a common or popular choice, people may be more likely to follow suit. This can be particularly effective in encouraging behaviors that may be seen as socially desirable, such as recycling or voting.

Chapter 6: Behavioral Economic Techniques

Behavioral economics and nudge theory have gained widespread attention in recent years for their ability to influence decision-making processes. This field combines insights from psychology, economics, and neuroscience to explain how people make decisions and what factors influence those decisions. Nudge theory, in particular, is a framework for designing interventions that influence people's behavior in predictable and beneficial ways.

The central Idea of nudge theory is that small, subtle changes to the environment or context in which people make decisions can have a significant impact on their behavior. These changes are often designed to make the preferred behavior the easiest or most attractive option, while still allowing people to make their own choices.

The term "nudge" was coined by Richard Thaler and Cass Sunstein in their influential book,

"Nudge: Improving Decisions About Health, Wealth, and Happiness." They argue that nudges can be used to help people make better decisions without restricting their freedom of choice. Instead of imposing mandates or regulations, nudges rely on people's natural tendencies and biases to guide them towards better outcomes.

Behavioral economics and nudge theory have been applied in a variety of domains, from public health and environmental policy to finance and marketing. For example, in the realm of public health, nudges have been used to encourage people to eat healthier foods, exercise more, and quit smoking. In finance, nudges have been used to increase retirement savings rates and encourage people to invest in socially responsible funds.

In this chapter, we will explore the key concepts and principles of behavioral economics and nudge theory, as well as how they can be applied to influence decisions and choices in various contexts. We will also examine the potential benefits and limitations of these approaches, and the ethical considerations involved in using nudges to influence behavior.

Behavioral economics is based on the idea that people don't always make rational decisions. Instead, they are influenced by a variety of cognitive biases and heuristics, which can lead to systematic errors in judgment. These biases and heuristics can be exploited by those who understand them to influence decision-making and shape behavior.

One of the key insights of behavioral economics is that people often have a strong aversion to losses, and will go to great lengths to avoid them. This can lead to irrational decision-making, such as holding onto a losing investment for too long in the hope of recouping losses. Another key insight is that people are often more influenced by the way information is presented to them than by the information itself. For example, people may be more likely to buy a product if it is presented as a limited-time offer or if it is framed as a gain rather than a loss.

Nudge theory is based on the idea that by making small changes to the way choices are presented, it is possible to influence behavior without resorting to coercion or mandates. Nudges are designed to be subtle, often leveraging behavioral economics principles, to encourage people to make choices that are in their best interest. For example, a cafeteria might rearrange its food options to make healthy choices more prominent and appealing, making it more likely that people will choose healthier options.

Behavioral economics and nudge theory provide powerful tools for influencing behavior, particularly when it comes to promoting positive outcomes like health, safety, and environmental sustainability. In the following sections, we will explore some of the most effective strategies for applying these theories in practice.

Nudge Theory is a concept in behavioral economics that suggests that people can be influenced to make certain decisions based on how choices are presented to them. The theory is based on the idea that people often make decisions that are not in their best interest, and that small changes to the way choices are presented can have a big impact on decision-making.

Nudge Theory was popularized in the book "Nudge: Improving Decisions About Health, Wealth, and Happiness" by Richard Thaler and Cass Sunstein. In the book, they argue that people can be influenced to make better decisions by making small changes to the way choices are presented to them. These changes are often referred to as "nudges."

The Idea behind Nudge Theory is to make it easier for people to make good decisions by presenting choices in a way that encourages them to make the best choice. This can be done by simplifying choices, providing information in a clear and concise way, or by framing choices in a way that makes one option more appealing than others.

Nudge Theory has been applied in a wide range of settings, from encouraging people to save more for retirement to improving public health outcomes. By using simple nudges, policymakers and organizations can help people make better decisions without limiting their freedom of choice.

Framing is a technique used to influence how people perceive and interpret information. The way a message is framed can have a significant impact on how it is received and interpreted. It is often used to shape public opinion or support for a particular policy or idea.

There are several ways to frame a message, including emphasizing the positive aspects of an idea or highlighting the negative consequences of not taking action. For example, a message about the benefits of a new policy might focus on the positive outcomes that will result, such as improved health or increased economic growth. Alternatively, a message might highlight the negative consequences of not implementing the policy, such as increased costs or a decline in quality of life.

Framing can also be used to create a sense of urgency or importance around an issue. By framing an issue as a crisis or an urgent problem that requires immediate action, it can motivate people to take action and support a particular policy or idea.

In order to effectively use framing in influence campaigns, it is important to understand the target audience and their values and beliefs. By tailoring messages to resonate with the audience's existing beliefs and values, it is more likely to be received positively and have the desired effect.

In addition, emotions play a significant role in decision making. People often make decisions based on how they feel, rather than solely on logic or reason. As a result, effective influence techniques often leverage emotions to encourage a desired behavior or decision.

One way to do this is through the use of emotional appeals, such as evoking fear, hope, guilt, or happiness. For example, an advertisement for a security system might play on the fear of a home invasion, while a charity appeal might evoke feelings of guilt or empathy for those in need.

Another way to influence emotions is through the use of framing. Framing is the way a message is presented or "framed" to influence how it is perceived. For example, a message that emphasizes the potential losses associated with a decision may elicit a stronger emotional response than one that emphasizes potential gains.

Understanding the role of emotions in decision making can be a powerful tool for those looking to influence others. By tapping into the right emotions and using effective framing techniques, it is possible to shape the way people think and act. However, it is important to use this power ethically and responsibly, and to consider the potential unintended consequences of any influence tactics used.

Choice architecture is the design of the environment in which people make choices. It involves structuring the options available to people in a way that nudges them towards a particular decision without restricting their freedom of choice. The aim of choice architecture is to make the desired choice the easiest or most appealing option.

For example, a company might want to encourage its employees to save for retirement. By changing the default option in their retirement plan from opt-in to opt-out, more employees are likely to start saving for retirement. This is because the default option is the one that requires the least effort, and people are more likely to stick with the default.

Another example of choice architecture is the use of social norms. People are more likely to conform to a particular behavior if they believe it is the norm. For instance, if a hotel places a sign in the bathroom asking guests to reuse their towels to help conserve water, it can be effective at promoting environmentally-friendly behavior. This is because guests may be more likely to comply with the request if they believe it is what most people do.

Framing refers to the way in which information is presented or "framed" in order to influence the way people interpret it. This can be done by highlighting certain aspects of the information and downplaying or omitting others, using particular words or phrases to convey a specific meaning, or presenting the information in a particular context that makes it more or less relevant to the audience.

One common example of framing is the way in which political issues are presented in the media. Depending on the political leanings of the media outlet, issues may be framed in a way that supports a particular political agenda or ideology. For example, a conservative-leaning media outlet may frame an issue around the need for individual responsibility and limited government intervention, while a liberal-leaning outlet may frame the same issue around the need for social justice and collective action.

Framing can also be used in advertising and marketing to influence consumer behavior. For example, a product may be framed as a luxury item with high status appeal, or as a practical and affordable choice for everyday use. The way in which the product is framed can impact the way consumers perceive its value and desirability.

In addition, framing can also be used in negotiations and conflict resolution to influence the outcome of the negotiation. By framing the negotiation in a particular way, negotiators can encourage the other party to see the situation from a certain perspective, making it more likely that they will agree to a particular proposal.

Priming is a psychological phenomenon where exposure to a stimulus can influence an individual's behavior or response to a subsequent stimulus. In other words, priming involves exposing someone to a certain idea or concept, which can then affect their behavior or decision-making.

For example, if someone is primed with images or words related to cleanliness, they may be more likely to choose a cleaning product when given a choice between cleaning and non-cleaning products. Similarly, if someone is primed with words related to aggression, they may be more likely to respond aggressively to a subsequent situation.

Priming can be used in influence techniques by strategically exposing individuals to certain stimuli to shape their attitudes, beliefs, and behavior. Advertisers, politicians, and other influencers use priming to shape public opinion and promote their agendas.

One example of priming in advertising is the use of celebrity endorsements. By associating a celebrity with a particular product, advertisers can prime consumers to associate positive qualities with that product, such as attractiveness or success.

In political campaigns, priming can be used to shape public opinion about a candidate or issue. For example, by repeatedly associating a candidate with words like "strong" or "honest," campaign strategists can prime voters to view that candidate in a positive light.

Chapter 7: Humor in Influence

Humor has always been a powerful tool for communication, and it can be particularly effective in influence campaigns. Humor can help to break down barriers, disarm people, and create a sense of connection between the communicator and the audience. When used strategically, humor can be a potent force in shaping attitudes and beliefs, making it an important consideration for anyone looking to influence others.

The use of humor In influence campaigns is not a new phenomenon. In fact, humor has been used as a tool for persuasion since ancient times. The ancient Greeks, for example, used satire and comedy to critique political leaders and social norms, and even the Bible contains examples of humorous stories that were used to convey moral lessons.

In modern times, humor has been used in a variety of influence campaigns, from political campaigns to advertising to social media campaigns. One of the reasons humor can be so effective is that it can be used to address difficult or sensitive topics in a non-threatening way. By using humor, communicators can help to reduce the psychological barriers that might otherwise prevent people from engaging with their message.

However, the use of humor in influence campaigns is not without its risks. Humor can be highly subjective, and what one person finds funny, another person may find offensive or inappropriate. Additionally, humor that is not carefully crafted can backfire and actually turn people off from the message being communicated. For these reasons, it is important for communicators to approach the use of humor in influence campaigns with care and intentionality.

Humor can also be used to build rapport and a sense of camaraderie between the persuader and the target audience. By using humor in a relatable way, the persuader can create a connection with the audience and establish a sense of trust. When people laugh together, it creates a bond between them, and this bond can be used to influence their attitudes and behaviors. For example, a politician may use self-deprecating humor to show that they are down-to-earth and relatable to voters, which can help build trust and support for their campaign. Additionally, humor can be used to defuse tension in a difficult situation or to address a sensitive topic in a non-threatening way, which can make the message more palatable to the target audience. Overall, humor can be a powerful tool in the arsenal of a persuader, as long as it is used appropriately and with the right audience in mind.

Humor can be a powerful tool for persuasion, as it can help to create positive emotions and build rapport between the communicator and the audience. When used effectively, humor can help to convey a message in a way that is engaging and memorable.

One way that humor can be used in influence campaigns is through the use of satire. Satire involves using humor to expose and ridicule human vices or shortcomings, often with the goal of encouraging change or reform. Satire can be particularly effective in influencing public opinion, as it allows the communicator to critique a particular issue or group without directly attacking them.

Another way that humor can be used in influence campaigns is through the use of parody. Parody involves using humor to imitate and exaggerate a particular style or genre, often for comedic effect. Parody can be used to draw attention to a particular issue or to make a political or social point.

Also, humor can be used in influence campaigns simply to entertain the audience and create positive associations with the communicator or the message. By using humor to create a positive emotional state, the communicator can help to increase the likelihood that the audience will be receptive to the message and take the desired action.

Humor can take many different forms, and understanding the different types of humor can be helpful in creating effective influence campaigns.

Here are some of the most common types of humor used in influence campaigns:

Satire: Satire involves using irony, sarcasm, and exaggeration to criticize and ridicule people or institutions. This type of humor is often used in political campaigns to highlight the shortcomings of opponents or to draw attention to important issues.

Parody: Parody involves using humor to imitate or mock something in a way that is funny or entertaining. This type of humor is often used to create memorable advertisements or to make fun of competitors.

Puns: Puns involve playing with words to create a humorous effect. This type of humor can be used to make a message more memorable or to lighten the tone of a serious message.

Irony: Irony involves using language to convey the opposite of what is expected. This type of humor can be used to create a sense of surprise or to highlight the absurdity of a situation.

Self-Deprecation: Self-deprecating humor involves making fun of oneself or one's own group. This type of humor can be used to create a sense of empathy with the audience or to poke fun at oneself before others have a chance to.

Understanding the different types of humor and their effects on the audience can be crucial in creating effective influence campaigns.

In the digital age, humor has taken on new forms and platforms, such as memes and social media. Memes, which are humorous images, videos, or text that spread rapidly online, have become a popular tool for influencing public opinion. They are often used to satirize politicians or social issues, and can quickly go viral if they strike a chord with audiences. For example, during the

2016 U.S. presidential election, memes were used extensively by both sides to ridicule opponents and spread propaganda.

Social media platforms have also become a hub for humorous content and satire, and influencers have taken advantage of this to sway public opinion. For instance, political comedians like John Oliver and Samantha Bee have amassed large followings on social media platforms by using humor to criticize political figures and institutions.

However, it is worth noting that humor can also be used in negative and harmful ways in the digital age, such as cyberbullying and the spread of hate speech disguised as humor. Therefore, it is important for those using humor in influence campaigns to be aware of these potential harms and use their influence responsibly.

Chapter 8: Neuro-Linguistic Programming

Neuro-Linguistic Programming (NLP) is a powerful communication and personal development tool that has been used for decades. It was created in the 1970s by Richard Bandler and John Grinder, who studied and modeled the communication and behavioral patterns of successful therapists such as Virginia Satir, Fritz Perls, and Milton H. Erickson.

NLP is based on the idea that our thoughts, emotions, and behavior are all interconnected and can be reprogrammed through language and communication. By understanding the structure and language patterns of successful communication and behavior, NLP can be used to create positive changes in oneself and others.

NLP has been used in various fields, including business, sports, therapy, education, and personal development. It is a powerful tool for communication, negotiation, persuasion, and influence.

In this chapter, we will explore the principles and techniques of NLP and how they can be used in the context of influence and persuasion. We will cover various NLP techniques that can be used to build rapport, establish credibility, and influence behavior. By the end of this chapter, you will have a basic understanding of NLP and its application in the field of influence and persuasion.

NLP offers a variety of techniques that can be used for influence. Some of the most commonly used techniques are:

 Anchoring: Anchoring is a powerful NLP technique used to influence and persuade people by establishing a reference point, or anchor, to which future decisions or actions are compared. The anchor can be anything from a word or phrase to a gesture, sound, or even a scent. Once established, the anchor can be triggered to evoke a specific response or behavior from the person.

Anchoring works by leveraging the human brain's tendency to rely on cognitive shortcuts, or heuristics, to make decisions. By establishing an anchor, the brain is primed to perceive subsequent information or stimuli in relation to the anchor, which can significantly influence the decision-making process.

For example, in a sales context, a salesperson might establish an anchor by showing a high-priced item first before showing a lower-priced item. The higher-priced item serves as the anchor, and the lower-priced item appears more affordable by comparison.

To effectively use anchoring, it's important to follow these steps:

Identify the desired behavior or response: The first step is to clearly define the behavior or response you want to elicit from the person. This could be anything from buying a product to agreeing to a proposal.

Establish the anchor: Choose a stimulus that will be used as the anchor, such as a specific word or phrase, gesture, or sound. Make sure the anchor is clearly associated with the desired behavior or response.

Create the context: The context in which the anchor is established is crucial. It should be a positive or neutral context, as negative emotions can interfere with the anchoring process.

Apply the anchor: Once the anchor is established, it can be applied to trigger the desired behavior or response. This can be done by repeating the anchor, or by presenting the anchor alongside the desired behavior or response.

Reinforce the anchor: Over time, the anchor can become stronger through repetition and reinforcement. By consistently applying the anchor in the desired context, the desired behavior or response can become more automatic and natural.

It's Important to note that anchoring should be used ethically and with the person's best interests in mind. Manipulating someone through anchoring can be seen as unethical and can damage trust and credibility.

Examples of anchoring can be found in various aspects of life, such as marketing, negotiations, and even personal relationships. Understanding the power of anchoring can help you to be more aware of when it is being used on you, and how to effectively use it in your own communication and persuasion efforts.

Reframing: Reframing is a powerful technique in NLP that involves changing the way people perceive a situation or experience by putting it in a different context or framing it differently. By doing so, you can alter the meaning or interpretation of a situation and influence the way people think or feel about it. Reframing can be used to change negative experiences into positive ones, resolve conflicts, and facilitate communication and understanding.

There are several types of reframing that can be used in NLP:

Context Reframing: This type of reframing involves changing the way a situation is framed or viewed by changing the context surrounding it. For example, if someone is feeling upset about a particular situation, a therapist might reframe it by asking them to view it from a different perspective or in a different context, which can help to change their emotional response.

Content Reframing: This type of reframing involves changing the way a situation is described or talked about by changing the words used to describe it. This can involve using more positive language to describe a negative situation or focusing on the positive aspects of a situation that might otherwise be seen as negative.

Outcome Reframing: This type of reframing involves changing the way a situation is viewed by focusing on the desired outcome rather than the current situation. This can be particularly helpful when dealing with difficult or challenging situations, as it can help to keep people motivated and focused on the end goal.

Frame Breaking Reframing: This type of reframing involves challenging the assumptions or beliefs that underlie a particular situation. This can be done by asking questions that challenge the status quo or by introducing new information or perspectives that challenge established beliefs or assumptions.

Identity Reframing: This type of reframing involves changing the way a person views themselves or their role in a particular situation. This can be particularly helpful in situations where a person feels stuck or unable to make progress, as it can help to shift their perspective and open up new possibilities for action.

Solution Reframing: This type of reframing involves shifting the focus from the problem to the solution. It involves helping people to reframe their thinking so that they are more focused on finding solutions rather than dwelling on the problem itself. This can be particularly helpful in situations where people feel overwhelmed or stuck and are struggling to find a way forward

Another type of reframing is positive reframing, which involves finding positive aspects in a negative situation or experience. This technique can be especially helpful in therapy and coaching contexts, where clients may be struggling with negative emotions and thoughts. By focusing on positive aspects, clients may be able to shift their perspective and gain a sense of empowerment. Another type of reframing is cognitive reframing, which involves changing the way we think about a situation. This can be done by questioning and challenging negative or limiting beliefs, and replacing them with more positive and empowering ones. Cognitive reframing can be useful in overcoming self-doubt, anxiety, and negative self-talk.

Social reframing is another type of reframing that involves changing the social context or framing of a situation. This can be done by changing the social norms, expectations, or cultural values that influence our perceptions and behaviors. Social reframing can be a powerful tool in promoting social change and challenging oppressive systems and structures.

Finally, experiential reframing involves changing the way we experience a situation through sensory or perceptual changes. This can be done by changing the environment, music, lighting, or other sensory stimuli that can influence our perceptions and emotions. Experiential reframing can be a useful tool in managing anxiety, depression, and other emotional challenges.

Reframing can be used in a variety of settings, including coaching, therapy, and communication.

Here are some examples of how reframing can be used:

In coaching: Reframing can be used to help clients shift their perspectives on a situation, identify new possibilities, and move forward with more positive energy and motivation.

In therapy: Reframing can be used to help clients overcome limiting beliefs and negative self-talk, and to reframe negative experiences in a more positive light.

In communication: Reframing can be used to resolve conflicts, facilitate understanding and empathy, and promote positive relationships.

To use reframing effectively, it is important to understand the person's current frame of reference and the meaning they attach to a situation or experience. You can then use language patterns and questions to help them see the situation from a different perspective or in a different context. For example, you could ask questions like:

"What if you looked at it from a different angle?"

"How might you see it differently if you looked at the positive aspects?"

"What would happen if you chose to see it in a different light?"

It is also important to be sensitive and respectful when using reframing, as it can be a delicate process that requires trust and rapport between the parties involved. With practice, however, reframing can be a powerful tool for influencing and transforming the way people think and feel about a situation or experience.

Mirroring and matching are techniques used in Neuro-Linguistic Programming (NLP) to establish rapport with others by subtly mimicking their body language, speech patterns, and behavior. This technique can be used to build trust and establish a connection with someone quickly, as people tend to feel more comfortable and at ease with those who are similar to them.

To use mirroring and matching, start by observing the other person's body language, speech patterns, and behavior. Pay attention to their posture, gestures, and tone of voice. Then, subtly mimic their behavior in a way that is natural and not too obvious.

For example, if the other person is leaning forward, you might lean forward as well. If they are using hand gestures, you might use similar gestures. If they are speaking in a calm and measured tone, you might adjust your own tone to match theirs.

It Is important to note that mirroring and matching should be done subtly and with intention. You don't want to come across as insincere or manipulative. The goal is to establish a connection and build rapport, not to mimic the other person to an extreme degree.

Another way to use mirroring and matching is to use similar language and phrasing to the other person. For example, if they use a certain phrase or word repeatedly, you might start using it as well. This can help establish a common ground and make the other person feel heard and understood.

Mirroring and matching can be a powerful tool for building rapport and establishing a connection with others. However, it should be used with care and in a way that is authentic and respectful.

Metaphors and stories are powerful tools in NLP that allow for effective communication and influence. They work by tapping into the unconscious mind, which processes information in a more creative and intuitive way than the conscious mind.

Metaphors are comparisons that highlight the similarities between two things that are not usually associated with each other. They allow us to convey complex ideas and emotions in a way that is easy to understand and relate to. In NLP, metaphors are used to help people see things from a different perspective and to create new ways of thinking about problems.

Stories, on the other hand, are a way of communicating information in a narrative format. They have been used for centuries to convey moral lessons, share experiences, and to create emotional connections with others. In NLP, stories are used to help people understand complex concepts, to create a sense of empathy, and to inspire change.

To effectively use metaphors and stories in NLP, it is important to understand the different types of metaphors and stories that can be used, as well as the techniques for crafting them.

One type of metaphor is the "isomorphic metaphor," which uses a parallel situation or object to represent a situation or object in the real world. For example, you might use the metaphor of a river to represent the flow of life or a journey.

Another type of metaphor is the "symbolic metaphor," which uses a symbol or image to represent a concept or idea. For example, a butterfly might be used to represent transformation or change.

When crafting a story, it is important to use sensory language to create a vivid and engaging experience for the listener. This involves using words that activate the five senses, such as sight, sound, smell, taste, and touch. The story should also have a clear beginning, middle, and end, and should be structured in a way that supports the intended message or lesson.

In order to use metaphors and stories effectively in NLP, it is also important to consider the context and the audience. Different metaphors and stories will resonate with different people, depending on their experiences, beliefs, and values. Therefore, it is important to tailor the language and imagery to the individual or group being addressed.

Metaphors and stories are powerful tools in NLP that can be used to create new ways of thinking about problems, to inspire change, and to create emotional connections with others. By understanding the different types of metaphors and stories and the techniques for crafting them, NLP practitioners can enhance their ability to communicate effectively and influence others.

Chapter 9: Rumor Campaigns

Rumor campaigns are a form of information warfare that seeks to spread false information or create doubt and confusion about a person, group, or idea. The ultimate goal of a rumor campaign is to shape public opinion or perception in a way that benefits the initiator of the campaign.

Rumor campaigns can take many forms, from spreading unfounded gossip and hearsay to the dissemination of outright falsehoods. They can be conducted by individuals, groups, or even entire governments. In recent years, the use of social media has made it easier than ever to spread rumors quickly and efficiently to large audiences.

Rumor campaigns are often used to sow discord and undermine social cohesion, but they can also be used to achieve more specific goals, such as discrediting political opponents or influencing the outcome of an election. They are particularly effective when they play into pre-existing biases and beliefs, or when they appear to come from a credible source.

It Is important to note that not all false information or rumors are part of a deliberate campaign. Rumors can also arise spontaneously as a result of misinterpretation, misunderstanding, or incomplete information. However, deliberate rumor campaigns are designed to exploit these natural tendencies and amplify their effects.

Rumor campaigns can be launched for various reasons, such as discrediting a political opponent, creating chaos and confusion, or promoting a particular agenda. These campaigns are often fueled by emotions and play on people's fears, insecurities, and biases. They can spread quickly through various channels, including social media, word of mouth, and even traditional media.

In order to launch an effective rumor campaign, it's important to identify a target audience and understand their values, beliefs, and fears. This can be done through research and analysis of social media trends, online forums, and other sources. Once the target audience has been identified, the next step is to craft a compelling story that resonates with them and triggers an emotional response.

One effective technique for launching a rumor campaign is to create a sense of urgency and scarcity. This can be done by spreading rumors about an impending disaster or crisis that can only be averted by taking a particular action. The action could be anything from buying a particular product to supporting a particular political candidate.

Another effective technique is to appeal to people's emotions and biases. This can be done by using strong language, evocative imagery, and provocative statements that tap into people's deepest fears and anxieties. For example, a rumor campaign could play on people's fears about immigrants or refugees by spreading rumors about crime and terrorism.

In order to ensure that the rumor campaign spreads quickly and effectively, it's important to leverage various channels, including social media, email, and word of mouth. The campaign should be designed to go viral, with people sharing and reposting the rumors without even realizing they are part of a coordinated campaign.

It's important to monitor and track the progress of the rumor campaign, and make adjustments as needed. This can be done by tracking social media mentions, monitoring online forums and chat rooms, and analyzing traditional media coverage. By monitoring the progress of the campaign, it's possible to fine-tune the message and adjust the tactics to ensure maximum impact.

Characteristics of Rumors:

Rumors have several distinguishing characteristics that differentiate them from other types of information. These include:

Uncertainty: Rumors often contain information that is uncertain or unverified, which makes them difficult to refute or confirm. This uncertainty also makes them more likely to be passed on, as people are often curious about the veracity of the information they are hearing.

Emotional Content: Rumors often contain emotionally charged content, such as stories of injustice, danger, or scandal. This emotional content can make the rumors more appealing to people, as they are more likely to be shared and believed if they tap into people's fears, hopes, or desires.

Simplicity: Rumors are often simple and easy to understand, which makes them more accessible to a wider audience. They can be conveyed through short, catchy phrases or simple stories, making them more memorable and shareable.

Source Ambiguity: The source of a rumor is often unclear or unknown, which can make it more difficult to trace and debunk. This ambiguity can also add to the allure of the rumor, as people are often more likely to believe something if they do not know who it came from.

Understanding these characteristics can be helpful in identifying and combating rumors, as it allows you to anticipate how they might be spread and what types of counter-messages might be effective in dispelling them.

Once the objectives and targets have been identified, the next step is to design a comprehensive campaign strategy. This includes creating a timeline for the campaign, identifying key messages and themes, determining the best channels for dissemination, and allocating resources appropriately. It's important to consider the potential impact of the rumor campaign on different groups of people and to tailor the strategy accordingly. Additionally, contingency plans should be developed in case the campaign encounters unforeseen obstacles or receives pushback.

Some important factors to consider when designing a rumor campaign strategy include understanding the target audience, crafting messages that resonate with their values and beliefs, and selecting the most effective channels for reaching them. It's also essential to monitor the campaign's progress and adjust the strategy as needed to ensure that it's achieving the desired results.

Chapter 10: Resisting Influence

To effectively resist influence campaigns, it's important to first understand how they work. Influence techniques can range from subtle persuasion tactics to outright manipulation, and they often rely on triggering automatic, unconscious thought processes.

One important concept to understand is cognitive biases, which are inherent flaws in our thinking patterns that can lead us to make irrational decisions. Influence campaigns may take advantage of these biases, such as the confirmation bias, where we tend to seek out information that confirms our existing beliefs, or the availability bias, where we give more weight to information that is more easily accessible.

Another key concept is social proof, which is the tendency to look to others when making decisions. Influence campaigns may use social proof by highlighting the popularity or endorsement of a product or idea.

Finally, it's important to be aware of the emotional appeal of influence campaigns. Many techniques may rely on fear, guilt, or other emotions to influence our decision-making.

By understanding these underlying concepts, we can begin to recognize and resist influence campaigns more effectively.

One key step to resisting influence campaigns is to be aware of common persuasion tactics used by influencers. Here are some common tactics to watch out for:

Scarcity: When influencers create a sense of urgency or scarcity around their product or message, it can lead people to make impulsive decisions. For example, a limited-time offer or a product that is "selling out fast" can create a fear of missing out (FOMO) that can be hard to resist.

Social Proof: When influencers use social proof, they rely on people's tendency to conform to the behavior of others. For example, if a product has a lot of positive reviews or if a message is shared widely on social media, people may be more likely to believe it or to follow along.

Authority: People are more likely to believe and follow those who are perceived as authoritative or knowledgeable. Influencers may use this to their advantage by highlighting their credentials or expertise in a particular area.

Likability: People are also more likely to be influenced by those they like or admire. Influencers may use humor, charisma, or other tactics to make themselves more likable or relatable to their audience.

Reciprocity: The principle of reciprocity suggests that people feel obligated to return a favor or a kind gesture. Influencers may use this by offering a free sample or a small gift, with the hope that people will feel compelled to reciprocate by purchasing their product or supporting their message.

Developing critical thinking skills is an effective way to resist influence campaigns. Critical thinking involves analyzing, evaluating, and interpreting information and arguments to make reasoned judgments. Here are some ways to improve your critical thinking skills:

Question assumptions: Be aware of your assumptions and biases, and ask yourself if they are justified. Don't take things at face value and always seek evidence to support claims.

Consider multiple perspectives: Be open to hearing different viewpoints and consider how they might inform your own beliefs. This can help you avoid confirmation bias and broaden your perspective.

Evaluate evidence: Look at the quality and reliability of the evidence presented to you. Consider the source of the information and whether it has been peer-reviewed or verified by multiple sources.

Practice skepticism: Be wary of claims that sound too good to be true or are not supported by evidence. Question authority and be willing to challenge conventional wisdom.

Use logic and reason: Analyze arguments and evidence using logic and reason rather than emotion. Evaluate claims based on their soundness and validity, rather than how they make you feel.

Staying informed: Keep up to date with the latest news and events related to the issue at hand. Stay informed about the different sides of the issue and seek out diverse perspectives.

Fact-checking: Verify the information you receive from various sources before accepting it as true. Look for reliable sources and fact-checking websites that can help you determine the accuracy of information.

Seeking professional help: If you are unsure about a decision or need additional information, seek help from professionals who are experts in the relevant field.

Researching the organization or individual behind the campaign: Investigate the background of the organization or individual behind the campaign. Look for information about their past activities and any controversies or scandals associated with them.

Building resilience is crucial for resisting influence campaigns. Resilience refers to the ability to adapt and recover from adverse situations. In the context of resisting influence campaigns, resilience involves developing a strong sense of self-awareness and critical thinking skills to help you recognize and resist manipulative tactics.

Here are some tips for building resilience:

Develop a strong sense of self-awareness: This involves understanding your values, beliefs, and biases. When you have a strong sense of self-awareness, you are less likely to be swayed by manipulative tactics that conflict with your values and beliefs.

Improve your critical thinking skills: Critical thinking skills help you analyze information objectively and make informed decisions. Some ways to improve your critical thinking skills include reading diverse perspectives, questioning assumptions, and considering multiple sources of information.

Practice mindfulness: Mindfulness involves being present and aware of your thoughts, feelings, and environment. When you are mindful, you are less likely to be reactive and more able to respond thoughtfully to manipulative tactics.

Build a support network: Surround yourself with people who support your values and beliefs. They can provide a sounding board and help you stay grounded when faced with manipulative tactics.

Take care of your physical and mental health: Good physical and mental health is crucial for building resilience. Make sure to exercise regularly, get enough sleep, eat a healthy diet, and practice self-care.

Chapter 11: Conclusion

After exploring the world of influence and the various techniques used in influence campaigns, it's clear that influence is an incredibly powerful tool that can be used for both good and bad. While there are many legitimate uses of influence, such as in advertising and politics, there are also many unethical uses that can manipulate people and harm individuals and society.

It's Important to be aware of these techniques, to recognize when they are being used on us, and to develop strategies to resist them. By being informed and mindful, we can protect ourselves and make more thoughtful and deliberate choices.

Furthermore, as we have seen throughout this book, influence is not just something that is done to us, but also something we can use to positively impact others. We can use these techniques ethically and responsibly to inspire, persuade, and encourage positive change.

The study of influence is an ongoing journey. It requires us to stay curious, informed, and critical of the messages we receive. By doing so, we can become more empowered and intentional in the choices we make, and work towards a more informed and just society.